Living in Two Economies

Living in Two Economies

Following Christ into the Marketplace

Bible Study Guide

For Individuals or Small Groups

Virginia G. Viola

To order additional copies of this book, contact:
Xlibris Corporation
1-888-795-4274
www.Xlibris.com
Orders@Xlibris.com
51550

Contents

DEDICATION

With Special Thanks to:

Dr. James D. Bruce

Former Professor of Electrical Engineering and Chief Information Officer
and Vice President for Information Systems at M.I.T.,
Former moderator and teacher at Park Street Church, Boston, MA.
Co-founder of Marketplace Network Inc, in Boston, MA
Current Professor of Electrical Engineering Emeritus and
Vice President for Information Systems Emeritus at M.I.T.

Thomas L. Phillips

Former CEO of Raytheon
Former Founder and President of Marketplace Network Inc, in Boston, MA
Former Adjunct Professor at Gordon Conwell Theological Seminary
whose teaching and modeling of Jesus' principles in a course at GCTS
made a deep impression on me as he led pastors, business people, and
seminarians in a dialogue around case studies and Jesus' teachings.

The teachings and modeling of these two men have deeply influenced the
way I and many others go to work and pursue our personal callings.

Acknowledgements

I am deeply appreciative of the writings of Randy Kilgore whose study guides provided a basis for many of us in to begin to integrate our personal faith in God with life at work in our various industries. Randy currently can be reached at *www.madetomatter.org*.

Many thanks Denise Thompson-Smith for her editing expertise and help in preparing this study for publishing.

Introduction

How do we work alongside people with whom we do not see eye to eye week after week? Daily following Christ in the marketplace often make us feel like we are living in two economies. Christians are required to live life aware of two realities. The first is in the tangible world where people live and work, and which God created and He told us to "tend to" (Genesis 2:15). The second is the spiritual world with its eternal perspective. In one economy, we seek to pursue God's call to "work it and take care of it (His Creation)" through our daily work with excellence and integrity in a world where we do not always see eye to eye with our colleagues and bosses. In the other economy, we seek to respond to Christ's lordship over all our lives, including workplace, family, community and church (Colossians 3:23). We often experience times when our personal faith clashes with the demands of our jobs and our roles in the public arena. The Bible affirms that all work, paid or unpaid, in all spheres of His creation matters to Him. Jesus Christ, praying to the Father and with His leadership team during His last night on earth, said *"I have brought You glory on earth by completing the work You gave me to do . . . As You sent me into the world, I have sent them into the world" (John 17:4, 18).*

How do we define success in terms that encompass all of life, not merely our career goals and accomplishments? Our goal is to develop a healthy work ethic rather than shifting our values in our work situations. The shift from driven ambition to a healthy work ethic, the shift from moral relativity to steadfast character, are some of the changes God wants to bring about as we live out our lives in these two economies.

Each of the 10 lessons includes an opening reflection for group discussion to open up the topic, some suggested biblical passages to read to stimulate your thinking, and some leaders notes to help your discussion and application of the texts. These lessons are designed to help the reader integrate biblical faith and daily life at work where so many people spend 40 to 60 hours a week. The Bible tells us God has entrusted His work since Creation into our hands (Genesis 2:15, Psalm 8:6), but how do we follow His calling in our pluralistic, relativistic world of the public arena? This study guide is designed to be a helpful tool for individuals or groups to read and discuss together as they seek to live out their calling from God.

Bible passages quoted are from the New International Version unless stated otherwise.

Background information for leaders and group members on all the passages referred to can be found in two volumes from InterVarsity Press:

New Bible Commentary (21st Century Edition)
ed. Gordon J. Wenham, J. Alec Motyer, Donald A. Carson and R. T. France
New Bible Dictionary (3rd Edition)
ed. I. Howard Marshall, A. R. Millard, J. I. Packer and Donald J. Wiseman

Getting the Most Out
of This Study

Suggestions for Individual Study

1. As you begin each study, ask God to speak to you through His Word and by His Spirit.

2. Have a Bible of your choice for your personal study. New International Version (NIV) or the New Living Translation (NLT) are both good translations for this purpose. If you have a study Bible, the additional notes will clarify the passage and historical background for you. You can always go online to get any passage at www.biblegateway.com.

3. Read the introduction to the topical study and respond to the personal reflection question or exercise. This will help you focus on God and on the theme of the study.

4. Each study deals with a topic and one or two Bible passages. Read and re-read the passage(s) to be studied. Quotes from the Bible are from the New International Version unless otherwise stated.

5. Write your answers to the questions in the spaces provided or in a personal journal. Writing can bring clarity and deeper understanding of yourself and God's Word. Write down in the margins any questions that come to mind.

6. Use the prayer suggestion to guide you in thanking God for what you have learned and to pray about the applications that have come to mind.

7. You may want to go on to the suggestion under "Now or Later", or you may want to use that idea for your next study.

Suggestions for Members of a Group Study

1. Come to your group prepared. Follow the suggestions for individual study mentioned above. You will find that careful preparation will greatly enrich your time spent in group discussion. The group is designed for an hour long study so it can be used by groups over breakfast or lunch.

2. Be willing to participate in the discussion. The leader of your group will not be lecturing. Instead, he or she will be encouraging the members of the group to discuss what they have learned. The leader will be asking the questions that are found in this guide.

3. Stick to the topic being discussed. Your answers should be based on the verses which are the focus of the discussion and not outside authorities, such as commentaries or speakers. This allows everyone to participate on equal ground.

4. Be careful not to dominate the discussion. We are sometimes so eager to express our thoughts that we leave too little opportunity for others to respond. By all means participate! but allow others to do so as well.

5. Expect God to teach you through the passage being discussed and through the other members of the group. Pray that you will have an enjoyable and profitable time together, but also that as a result of the study you find ways that you can take action individual and or s a group.

6. Remember that anything said in the group is considered confidential and should not be discussed outside the group unless specific permission is given to do so.

7. Leaders Notes at the end of each lesson will provide additional reflections and background information on many of the questions.

Enjoy the journey together!!

Ginny Viola

Lesson 1

Why Work?

Does our personal work really matter to God? Are all jobs automatically given the nod by God? Is God interested in more than our inner personal life?

God is our model for why we work and how we fit into His goals for creation and culture. God worked and created us in His own image to join Him in work. The word "work" and "worker" occurs over 600 times in the New International Version of the Bible, translated from several Greek and Hebrew words for work. There seems to be no apparent difference between the word's used of *God's work*, or *man's work*, or the differentiation between "sacred" and "secular" work in the Old and New Testaments.

Group Reflection:

Write down a word or phrase, other than your name that identifies you.

Share your answers and see how many of these phrases describe what you do for work?

Individual Reflection:

Why do people go to work? Why do *you* go to work?

Read Genesis 1 and Genesis 2:15 and Psalm 8 and observe how we see God at work.

1. What kind of work did God perform in Creation? What different occupations and skill-sets would we need today to accomplish these tasks or to begin to copy what God did?

2. Why did God create human work in Genesis 1:27-28 and 2:15?

Read Psalm 8: 1-6

3. How did this political leader (King David) view the relationship between God's work and man's work?

4. How does this make you view yourself and your work?

5. How does this affect how you view other people with whom you work?

Prayer:

Thank God this week daily for:

- Creating you in His image to be a worker modeled after Him
- Being God's co-worker as you do your work in all arenas of your life
- Being a partner with God in shaping your culture

Now or Later:

1. How does Jesus reflect on His work?

   - John 5:17
   - John 17:4

2. What made work meaningful for Paul in Colossians 3:17?

For Leaders:

Notes on Question 1: Possible jobs needed for creation might be: architect, biomedical expert, architect water systems engineer, artist, landscape designer, farmer, environmentalist, etc.

Notes on Question 2: Work is a God-ordained function. All humans are created in His image to be a worker like Him and work with Him. Genesis 1:28—"fill the earth and subdue it; and have dominion." This is the first job description and it comes from God. Consider Psalm 8. Human labor is part of the divine creative enterprise. Note: No other religion holds to a belief in a God who works. God has designed all human beings and chosen to work with and through them to manage and develop His creative enterprise.

Notes on Question 3: Ever since Genesis 3 and man's chosen rebellion against God, work is filled with challenges and human conflicts, but work is still good and God is still sustaining His creation. We assume that since sin entered the sphere of creation, there will be no perfect job this side of heaven. (Romans 1:20-24, 8:18ff)

What are some of the fallen aspects of the nature of work?

Human beings were intended to subdue the earth for God's glory but instead sought to exploit it for themselves.

Work is mental and physical toil. Labor is tiring, frustrating, and monotonous.

Work relationships are spoiled: Conflict between labor and management, companies and clients, as well as disharmony in the workplace, are all examples of this. Whenever human beings are treated as mere tools of production, the fallen nature of humanity is operative.

Identity and social status tied to a person's job cultivate attitudes of pride, envy and insecurity.

Work has been redeemed from the effects of man's rebellion by Jesus Christ. Through the redemption brought about by the death of Christ, work as blessing prevails over work as curse. The fact that the eternal Son of God worked at a carpenter's bench is an extraordinary testimony to the sanctity of common work. Paul, too, set an example of honest labor by working as a tentmaker.

Notes on Questions 4 and 5: Not only am I created in God's image to be a worker like Him, but so are my colleague and neighbor at work. He or she is also someone for whom Jesus died whether they know it or not. Our colleagues have great value to God.

More Background for the Curious

Some biblical assumptions that might help provide a framework in which each of us might ask God questions about whether our work, or our colleagues' work, matters to Him:

a. God is interested and engaged in all His creation all the time. Therefore God is at our workplaces before we get there and also there when we leave. We can partner with Him in what He is doing, but we do not have to make things happen for God. We have only to be His instrument. (Psalm 8:6; Colossians 1:15-18, Proverbs 8:14-23 Etc.)

b. All our colleagues, including boss and employees, are created in the image of God with eternity in their hearts. (Ecclesiastes 3:11-14; Psalm 139)

c. Work has been entrusted into the hands of mankind (not just Christians). God's Word can equip us to do our work according to the designer's manual. God takes up residence in humans who have come into a personal relationship with Him. But He also uses those outside of His followers to accomplish His purposes, such as King Cyrus of Persia (Psalm 8:6; Ephesians 2:10; Isaiah 5:1-6).

d. God has given humans a free will, with all the risks that entails (Romans 1:20-24). The longer one chooses to walk with God, he/she will know more *how* to work, *what* to choose to do for work, and how to *make a difference* in the relationships at work.

e.   God's work of redeeming creation involves paid work (the area of focus of this study), community, family, volunteer, and church work. God's call to different individuals will involve roles in many or all of these areas. God works His call out in every biblical character differently, so we can assume He will work the "mix" in our lives uniquely too. (Psalm 8:6; Colossians 3:17; Luke 12:42-48)

Now or Later for leaders: Paul worked to please his boss Jesus. It was Jesus' Annual Review that motivated him. Work is to be done as a service to Christ. Paul wrote: "Slaves, obey in everything those who are your earthly masters, not with eye-service, as men-pleasers, but in singleness of heart, fearing the Lord. Whatever your task, work heartily, as serving the Lord and not men, knowing that from the Lord you will receive the inheritance as your reward. You are serving the Lord Christ." (Colossians 3:22-24) Work is to be part of our sacred stewardship as believers, and in this vital sense all our jobs come within the realm of the sacred. Exodus 31 provides a beautiful example in which the work of craftsmen and laborers in constructing "the tent of meeting" is the result of God's gift of His Spirit. Similarly, the New Testament concept of the priesthood of all believers implies that all our work is a spiritual service.

Lesson 2

How Do I Define Success?

Introduction

How different people define success determines the course they chart for their lives. What we define as success sets up our expectations, and we plan and work and even sacrifice to achieve that goal. Meaning, purpose, and success are all tied up together. Businesses have recognized this truth for years, making huge investments in trying to get workers committed to a mission and vision statement. The hope is that workers will become so focused on the objective—the corporate measure of success—that it will shape not only the nature of their labor, but also how much they're willing to sacrifice to achieve it.

Group Reflection:

How does our culture measure success in people? The answer can be how you measure whether others are successful, or measures you applied to yourself. Try to think about what makes *you* think someone is successful. Feel free to refer to media or advertisements you have observed recently.

Individual Reflection:

How would you define success for yourself?

Read Ecclesiastes 1:12-2:26

1. What do you know about the writer of this book? (his day job, the kind of work he did, his season of life)

2. What kinds of accomplishments had this man achieved?

3. What different ways had this gifted person sought to find meaning or success in his life?

Read Ecclesiastes 3:11-14.

1. Ecclesiastes (translated Teacher/Preacher) was considered successful by the standards of his culture. Why did Ecclesiastes feel meaning and success in life included more than just the work arena?

2. What do we know about God's intention for work from Genesis 2:15?

3. What had David learned about work both from God and from life experiences in Psalm 8:6?

4. How does Ecclesiastes attitude toward meaningful life and meaningful work compare with David's? What is similar and/or different?

5. What conclusions did Ecclesiastes come to about success and meaning in life?

   - Ecclesiastes 3:11-14

   - Ecclesiastes 5:18-20

   - Ecclesiastes 12:13-14

6. What role did work play in his understanding of success?

7. What are some benchmarks you would use in describing success for yourself?

Prayer:

This week, start each day thanking God for who He is:

- Omniscient (knows everything),
- Omnipresent (is everywhere),
- Omnipotent (has all power over all His creation).

In addition:

- Give Him your plans, your schedule for the day and week.
- Pray through your daytimer.
- Ask Him to anoint your plans or give you wisdom to change them.

Finally, be prepared for God's interruptions.

Now or Later:

Read Genesis 39. If you were Joseph's prayer partner, would you consider Joseph successful at this point in his day job? If Joseph came before God at this point for his Annual Review, what do you think God would have said to him and about him? Joseph's job description changes several times over his lifetime, from shepherd to slave to ultimately an international grain dealer and international humanitarian. If you were Joseph, how would you have evaluated your success in life at each of those seasons?

OR

Write an epitaph you would like for your life and legacy.

For Leaders:

Notes for the Group Reflection: As we look at advertisements and media reports, or listen to conversations around the water cooler at work, messages we hear are things like: To whom are you related? In which zip code do you live? 'What kind of car do you drive? What position do you hold at work or how many direct reports do you have? What do you do for leisure/travel? What clothes/labels you wear?

Notes on Questions 1 and 2: *Ecclesiastes* is probably written about Solomon as stated in 1:21, *'The Teacher, was king over Israel in Jerusalem''*. (Read the Introduction to the book of Ecclesiastes in the one Volume IVP Bible Commentary for more information). The book is part of the *Wisdom Literature* genre (like *Proverbs* and *Job*) which write about practical living rather than theology. The king/CEO was trying to make sense out of life this side of heaven, and the problem of evil and death, and what makes our daily work significant or satisfying. On the first reading of this book, one catches his despair and sense of futility in his life's accomplishments. Ecclesiastes 1-2 reveals a man who had multiple skill-sets, excelled in everything he took on, and who was still looking for contentment and meaning in the midst of multiple "successes" by the culture's criteria. He had unlimited funds for furnishings and pleasure; top position in the organization; and good team building skills in international relations. He excelled in construction, beautification, and water management. He made the court scholars part of the royal culture and had any woman he wanted. On the negative side, Solomon used women for his pleasure and used both men and women as slaves for his work. Every whim was satisfied yet he still found contentment and significance elusive[1].

Notes on Question 3: The bottom line for the author of *Ecclesiastes* is that life without God will always come up short in providing satisfaction for longer than a moment. The reason he gives is that God has put eternity into our hearts and the hearts of all humans (*Ecclesiastes 3:11*). Sin may have flawed God's original design for work and relationships and life, but each human is still in the image of God. Augustine and Pascal both wrote of "a God-shaped vacuum that only God can fill. Without a personal, daily relationship with God, the human heart will not be content or find meaning in work or other areas of life. God has designed each of us to find our identity in Him first and then to reflect that identity in the various areas of our lives. The teacher/king concludes that God wants us to enjoy the good gifts He gives to us in daily life but never let them become substitute for trusting in Him. *"Here is what I have seen to be good and fitting: to eat, to drink and enjoy oneself in all one's labor in which he toils under the sun during the few years of his life which God has given him; for this is his reward. Furthermore, as for every man to whom God has given riches and wealth, He has also empowered him to eat from them and to receive his reward and rejoice in his labor; this is the gift of God. For he will not often consider the years of his life, because God keeps him occupied with the gladness of his heart." (Ecclesiastes 5:18ff)*. The bottom line for Ecclesiastes was*: "Now all has been heard; here is the conclusion of the matter: Fear God and keep his commandments, for this is the whole duty of man. For God will bring every deed into judgment, including every hidden thing, whether it is good or evil."(Ecclesiastes 12:13ff)*.

Notes on Questions 6 and 7: Although David wrote some psalms that showed similar despair over life issues as does Ecclesiastes, here is an upbeat affirmation by David (also a political leader) who saw human work as shared dominion with the creator, even after the Fall. That meant that human work mattered to God both in what was done and how it was done. So just as King David marveled that God had entrusted His work into our hands (Psalm 8:6), work takes on great significance, Ecclesiastes affirms, when our lives are lived in response to His calling and design on our lives. Our work and relationships take on new meaning when success is defined by God's terms, rather than our

---

[1]   For a current example of a modern day Ecclesiastes, see Bob Buford's book *Half Time* where he describes his personal journey from success to significance. *At Amazon.com or at www.bobfuford.com.*

culture's. God's criteria are: am I becoming who God has designed me to be (the same for each of us in our character), and am I doing what God has called me to do (unique for each of us in our work, paid or unpaid)? While we are all called to become better image-bearers of Jesus' character, our work callings will be different, and will involve the different areas in each our lives (work, family, church, etc.) and will change with the seasons of life in which we find ourselves.

A Postscript on Solomon who experienced great success in his culture: God revealed his Life Review of Solomon after 40 years as king and world leader in international relations. It is interesting to compare God's review of Solomon with the reviews of Solomon's contemporaries. After Solomon started out his years of leadership walking with God, he then settled into his culture. *"He (Solomon) did the same for all his foreign wives, who burned incense and offered sacrifices to their gods. The LORD became angry with Solomon because his heart had turned away from the LORD, the God of Israel, who had appeared to him twice. Although he had forbidden Solomon to follow other gods, Solomon did not keep the Lord's command. So the LORD said to Solomon, "Since this is your attitude and you have not kept my covenant and my decrees, which I commanded you, I will most certainly tear the kingdom away from you and give it to one of your subordinates. Nevertheless, for the sake of David your father, I will not do it during your lifetime. I will tear it out of the hand of your son." (1 Kings 11:8ff)* While building international alliances through multiple marriages, he led his people and his family away from following their covenant with God. He affected everyone in his sphere of influence.

Lesson 3

Putting First Things First

Introduction

Listen in on a dialogue that Jesus had with a wealthy young man who came to Him with a question. Jesus answered his question with another question, which He often did to help his listeners get some insight.

Group Reflection:

Why do people in every culture and nation, in every period of history, seem to ask questions about how to have eternal life or think about God-questions relating to meaning and purpose in life?

Individual Reflection:

What question would you like to ask Jesus today if He appeared at your job or home ready for a chat?

Read Mark 10:17-31

1. In Mark 10:17-23, what do we learn about this young man? (His family, his community, and his roles)

2. What was his question and what do you think led him to ask it?

3. Comparing the young man's answers to Jesus about the Ten Commandments with the list in Exodus 20:1-17, what differences do you notice? What was left out?

4. In Mark 10:23-31, why were the disciples confused by Jesus teachings on wealth and resources?

5. What do you think Jesus is saying to His followers about wealth and resources?

6. What is the hardest thing for you to trust God for and why?

Prayer:

Praying with the writer of Proverbs 30:7-9:

> *"Two things I ask of you, O LORD; do not refuse me before I die: Keep falsehood and lies far from me; give me neither poverty nor riches, but*

give me only my daily bread. Otherwise, I may have too much and disown you and say, 'Who is the LORD?' Or I may become poor and steal, and so dishonor the name of my God."

Praying to Jesus:

- Here is my mind. Inform it.
- Here is my will. Conform it to yours.
- Here is my heart, continue to transform it until it reflects Your heart and mind for my life, my work, and this world.

Now or Later:

Read Psalm 73, and observe how the writer, Asaph, reflects on his barriers to trusting God and how material wealth fits in to his relationship with God.

Read Luke 16:1-17. Jesus often spoke about money. Here he commends a shrewd steward in his use of money and its influence in a parable and then Jesus teaches from it.

For Leaders:

Notes on Questions 1, 2 and 3: We watch Jesus attempting to help the young man move through some barrier(s) that were preventing him from integrating his personal faith and daily life. Once again, we observe Jesus responding uniquely to an individual who comes to Him. Jesus, again starting where the young man was, knew what his deeper "heart" questions were, even though unstated.

We listen in on a young man from a wealthy family, well-connected to temple culture, trying to do what is expected of him in life, given his roles. He knew that somehow "good" character and eternal life tied together. But where was the "bar" to measure what is good enough? "What must I *do to get* eternal life?" Show me the list. Jesus' answer at first looks like a tease. *Obey the commandments.* When asked which ones, Jesus gives a partial list of the Ten Commandments (known by heart by every Jewish person), a list of things one can do to check off. Jesus left out *"Thou shall not covet"*, a heart commandment that is harder to check off. In addition, the foundational commandments in Exodus 20 were left out that began with loving God first which is another heart commandment. *"I am the LORD your God, who brought you out of Egypt, out of the land of slavery." You shall have no other gods before me. "You shall not make for yourself an idol in the form of anything in heaven above or on the earth beneath or in the waters below. You shall not bow down to them or worship them; for I, the LORD your God, am a jealous God, punishing the children for the sin of the fathers to the third and fourth generation of those who hate me, but showing love to a thousand generations of those who love me and keep my commandments." (Exodus 20:2ff)* Jesus is saying "First things first". Start with the heart relationship with God who then can shape our values and our choices, as we begin to love what God loves and value what God values in ourselves and in others. Jesus shows He was not trying to tease or trick this young man, but wanting to help him gain some self-insight. Jesus did not come to condemn but to make whole. And He does not force Himself on anyone. Mark tells us *"Jesus looked at him and loved him. "One thing you lack" . . . (Mark 10:21).*

Notes on Question 4: Jesus goes on to tell the confused disciples that they will be personally looked out for by God. *"No one who has left home or brothers or sisters or mother or father or children or fields for me and the gospel will fail to receive a hundred times as much in this present age (homes, brothers, sisters, mothers, children and fields—and with them, persecutions) and in the age to come, eternal life". (Mark 10:29ff)* Jesus seems to be saying that the issue is not the giving up of family (and inheritance) or fields (business in an agrarian economy) but focusing on first things first, giving God first place and giving Him the control seat in our lives. When God is the Lord and not just an activity or section of our lives, He can not only transform us in our character but also shape our values and decisions about the rest of our lives as well.

Jesus shows us again His intimate knowledge of us as individuals. He seeks to help this young man move beyond his personal barriers to an intimate relationship with the God he professes to follow. Jesus says the one thing lacking was *"If you want to be perfect, go, sell your possessions and give to the poor, and you will have treasure in heaven. Then come, follow me." When the young man heard this, he went away sad, because he had great wealth." (Mark 10:22).* Why would Jesus tell him to give up all he had, when Jesus had not asked that of anyone else in the gospels? Yet three gospel writers record this conversation, followed by the consternation of His leadership team. In fact, Jesus often praised wise managers and successful business people in His teachings. To help this man find the answer to his heart-cry for meaning and purpose in life, Jesus is trying to free him from himself and his personal barrier. His identity was so rooted in his wealth and perhaps in the lifestyle connected with his wealth, that he was stuck until the crutch or substitute god was removed, and God was allowed His rightful place. While the man went away sad, we know Jesus will always be there if and when the young man decides to respond differently. Jesus never gives up on us or anyone else this side of heaven.

Lesson 4

Finding Balance in a Demanding Workplace

Introduction

How did Jesus model life-balance in a demanding workplace? He had a three year window to train 12 young leaders who were ex-fisherman, former tax collectors, etc. to take over His mission. His business plan targeted the whole world. What is more, the clients were at their door 24/7 and there was no letting up. How did Jesus handle the pressure on Himself and on his young team in training? We know at the end of His life He said He had finished the work the Father had given Him to do. (John 17:4) He seemed to be at peace with the fact that He had not met everyone's needs and requests. Every need did not constitute a call on His life, at least not one to be met by Jesus directly.

Group Reflection:

When have you experienced a time of burnout or exhaustion, and what caused it?

Individual Reflection:

What are some ways you experience rest, leisure and/or refreshment in your life?

Read Mark 6

1. What had been going on in the lives of the leadership team in Mark 6:1-13? What successes? What pressures?

2. What had happened to their colleague John the Baptist in Mark 6:14-29?

3. What kinds of needs does Jesus meet in the lives of His fledgling leadership team in Mark 6:30-32?

4. What does Jesus model for them and teach about interruptions to their plans in Mark 6:33-44, 52?

5. Jesus initiates a second period of rest and refreshment and a teaching moment in Mark 6:45-52. What does Jesus model for them and teach them in finding balance amid the pressures and demands?

6. For your own pursuit of balancing life's demands, what do you take away from Mark 6? What are you sensing God is saying to you about:

- your relationship with Him

- your priorities

- your choices this month

Prayer:

Lord Jesus, I give you my plans and schedule this week. I ask you to anoint my plans or change them. Give me wisdom to make wise choices and decisions. Overrule the circumstances by your sovereign power that you will be honored by me and through me this week.

When this week will you be spending time with Jesus: listening to Him through the Word and prayer, reviewing your schedule each day, talking over the past joys and frustrations, anticipating the opportunities and/or fears? As you ask Him to anoint your plans or change them and then look for God even in the interruptions. Take time for fellowship with others also on a journey with Jesus. Be refreshed and stretched and share how you are learning to trust Him in new ways in your daily life.

Now or Later:

Read 1 Kings 18-19. What were some successes Elijah experienced at this time in his life? What kinds of demands were on his life? What do you learn from Elijah's experience with burnout, its causes and effects? How did God work in Elijah's life to refresh him and give him new insight?

For Leaders:

Notes on Question 3: Taking time to be with the 12 was Jesus first response to the many demands. He listened to them, rejoiced with them over what they had experienced and learned, and probably answered their questions. Then due to the demands of the crowds, He initiated a time alone with the 12 for food, rest and time together. Jesus affirmed the need for time out from constant work, as valuable as their work was. Sustainable living has required rhythms of work and rest ever since creation. God rested after his creative work, not because He was tired but to enjoy His work. (Genesis 2:2-15) Sin has resulted in toilsome work for all humans (Genesis 3), but we too need some time to sit back and enjoy the results of our labors and to enjoy our relationship with the God who has made it all possible and meaningful. Rest is not for left over time of our lives but part of the sacred rhythms of life God has designed for us. Jesus models that for us as He lives day in and day out with the 12 for three years.

Notes on Question 4: Jesus intermingled teaching experiences with times of rest and reflection. He could have fed the 5,000 people Himself but wanted to teach the 12 about His power over nature in a way that let them participate in the mission . . . When the 12 could only think of sending the crowds away to find food after a long day, Jesus wanted them to share in the experience of feeding the people. He also expected them to grow in their faith in Him as "God with us". Jesus said, *"You give them something to eat." They said to him, "That would take eight months of a man's wages! Are we to go and spend that much on bread and give it to them to eat?" "How many loaves do you have?" he asked. "Go and see." When they found out, they said, "Five—and two fish." Then Jesus directed them to have all the people sit down in groups on the green grass. So they sat down in groups of hundreds and fifties. Taking the five loaves and the two fish and looking up to heaven, he gave thanks and broke the loaves. Then he gave them to his disciples to set before the people. He also divided the two fish among them all. They all ate and were satisfied, and the disciples picked up twelve basketfuls of broken pieces of bread and fish." (Mark 6:37ff)*

Notes on Question 5: Jesus initiated another period of rest by sending the 12 by boat across the large lake away from the crowds. Jesus then let them experience a frightening squall while crossing the lake. While walking across the water, Jesus then came to speak to them about their fears for safety, *"Take courage! It is I. Don't be afraid." Then he climbed into the boat with them, and the wind died down. They were completely amazed, for they had not understood about the loaves; their hearts were hardened."* (Mark 6:50) Initiating rest and then interruptions were all intentioned by Jesus to teach the 12 to trust Him in new ways and to get them to realize how worthy He was of their trust in real life experiences. The key was following Jesus' cues and His lead in the daily rhythms of work and rest.

Notes on Question 6: When we accepted Christ as our personal Savior and Lord, we began a journey to make Him Lord of our lives as well. As long as we're seeking to grow in our relationship with Him, God honors our efforts. When we surrender to the demands of this world and ignore His demand for first place in our hearts, we will be perpetually out of balance.

Lesson 5

Learning from the Master to Manage Stress

Introduction

Have you ever found yourself wondering why, if you are trusting God to the best of your ability, you still are experiencing the effects of stress in your life? Stresses from our workplaces can seem relentless due to the pace, financial duress, relationships with customers or colleagues or vendors, and even fear of failure or job loss in a changing economy. Then, if we add the stress that comes from wanting to care for family (and friends) whether near or far, the list grows. If God is sovereign and loving, why doesn't He change our circumstances to relieve our stresses?

Group Reflection:

What are the main stressors in your life at this time? Are they mainly from your work-life or your personal life outside of work?

Individual Reflection:

What are some ways you respond to stress?

Read Matthew 26:30-64

1. What are the circumstances that are causing stress to Jesus in this passage?

2. Who are the people causing stress in Jesus' life and how?

3. What options did Jesus have for responding to the circumstances and people that were making life hard for Him at this time?

4. How did Jesus respond to these stresses and disappointments?

5. What was His part? The Father's part?

6. What are you learning from observing Jesus that will help you handle the stress points in your life at this time?

Prayer:

As you go throughout the day, distracted by your stress points, practice this prayer to Jesus:

- Thee I adore . . . (*Your omniscience, omnipotence, omnipresence . . .*)

- Lord, have mercy . . . . (*Forgive me . . . Help me . . . .*)

- Into Thy hands (I put my *stressors, which are:* . . . .

Now or Later:

Read Nehemiah 1-2:16 and observe the stressors in his life from circumstances and people "on the job". What part did prayer play in his choices and what part did his actions play?

For Leaders:

Notes on Question 1: Jesus was stressed out "big time" in the garden of Gethsemane. (Matthew 26:36ff). This was His last night on earth. His leadership team was in a fragile state, having been treated unjustly by local leaders, both the religious and political. Jesus' life had been threatened. There was no support system left as His leadership team fell asleep while praying with Him. And then there was all that pain He would be facing very soon on the cross. We see Jesus physically and emotionally overwhelmed even though He was God in human form. Agitated and sweating drops of blood, wishing He could change His circumstances, how does Jesus respond? *"Then he said to them, 'My soul is overwhelmed with sorrow to the point of death. Stay here and keep watch with me.' Going a little farther, he fell with his face to the ground and prayed, 'My Father, if it is possible, may this cup be taken from me. Yet not as I will, but as you will.'* Jesus asked three times for relief. There was no immediate answer from His Father to the three requests.

Notes on Question 2: Jesus' leadership team let him down by falling asleep and not praying with Him. Religious and political leaders falsely accused Him and would go on to put him through three mock trials. His Father seemed absent and unresponsive. As Jesus was physically and emotionally exhausted, He was very much alone.

Notes on Question 3: Jesus had other options at His disposal. He goes on to say He could speak the word to retaliate and/or choose to relieve the pressure at the same time by opting not to follow through on the Father's plan: *"Do you think I cannot call on my Father, and He will at once put at my disposal more than twelve legions of angels?"* Jesus could speak the word as He often did to heal and free a person or to change a person's circumstances. But Jesus' larger vision was to play His unique role in God's larger agenda. Jesus' role was unique in what His death on the cross could accomplish for forgiveness of all humans. *"But how then would the Scriptures be fulfilled that say it must happen in this way?"* Jesus decided that the Father's agenda was more important than a stress-free life. We are also told that there was an inner joy in being in tune with God's agenda, even in the stress-filled times. (Hebrews 12:2)

Notes on Question 6: Jesus knows what stresses us and wants us to talk with Him regularly about these concerns. He wants us to remember His promises of love and provision and power. Yes, He can and might change the circumstances causing the stress. He wants the freedom to use us to accomplish His agenda which may mean "keeping on keeping on". He wants us to trust His love and power to accomplish His agenda in ways often unknown to us. He may want to do some "character development" and work on our shadow sides to make us each more like Him so the world can see Him more clearly in us and through us. He will provide joy on the journey, a day at a time. So let us keep our eyes on Him this week and not grow weary . . .

Thee I adore . . . .
Lord, have mercy . . . .
Into Thy hands . . . .

Lesson 6

Resisting the Urge to Compromise at Work

Introduction

How do we learn to live day by day with integrity in a culture that is constantly trying to draw us into choices that conflict with our values? Many people want us just to "go with the flow". When do we join in? When do we decide it is time to take a stand? In what parts of the office culture can we be flexible in our choices? Daniel is a refreshing role model. In his life we see how one godly young man and his three friends made a variety of choices.

Group Reflection:

When have you found yourself making a hard choice at work in recent weeks? What principles were involved? What relationships? What was the outcome?

Individual Reflection:

When have you found it hard to stand up for a principle at work? When have you found it hard to "build consensus" in a team situation?

Read Daniel 1

1. What was Daniel's background and life experience as we first learn about him in Daniel 1:1-6?

2. What recent experiences of Daniel (and his three friends) would have made him vulnerable to compromise in his new job? Note Daniel 1:1-6.

3. It what ways did Daniel choose to fit in with his culture? When did he choose to not "go with the flow"?

4. It what ways did Daniel's actions show respect for his boss and company policies? How and when did he choose to take a stand? What were the risks?

5. How did Daniel manage to keep an intimate walk with his God when he left Israel and home as a teenager?

6. What resources did God give Daniel to act with integrity and wisdom under pressure? (see also Daniel 2:16ff and 3:16)

7. What tools and resources has God given you so far? How does God want you to use them on the job and elsewhere in your life?

8. What can you begin to do this week to take advantage of God's resources in your life to help you live in what can often seem like a hostile environment?

Prayer:

This week thank Jesus for the resources He has given you to work alongside people with whom you do not see eye to eye. Name the people and/or conflicts with whom you are struggling. Ask Him to fill you with His Spirit and give you wisdom to respond to Him and not just react to the situation this week.

Now or Later:

Read Genesis 32 to 47 quickly, taking notice of several challenges on the jobs Joseph held. In what situations of Joseph's life would it have been tempting to compromise and make different choices?.

Leaders Notes:

Notes on Questions 1 and 2: How did Daniel end up as a direct report to the king? Daniel and his three other teenage friends were part of a group taken to Babylon through a hostile takeover of Israel in the 6th c BC. Teenagers of royal families were prime targets to take to the capital for indoctrination and training for leadership positions. We do not have much information on Daniel's reflections on these questions. We can only deduce his thoughts from his behavior. God opened doors for Daniel. God also gave Daniel brains, looks, people-skills and a capacity to walk through change well. But we also see Daniel choosing to be excellent in his studies and job training. He won the heart of his first boss not only by giving 100% of himself to the training, but also by letting the boss know that he was eager to see the boss succeed as well. When it came time to disagree with his boss, the trust by his boss was not an issue. Nature, nurture and God's sovereign hand all were part of Daniel's success.

Notes on Question 3: Once Daniel was moving up in leadership training, how did he withstand pressure to compromise and yet serve his boss? An additional gift to Daniel was the friendship of three friends who also wanted to follow their God and still be excellent in their new roles in Babylon. Can't you imagine their evening conversations about how they processed the day's activities and their studies? They decided they would go along with the new names and with understanding the new culture and its history, but would draw the line at eating palace food. While it is not stated, the Jewish food laws were probably being violated. Certain meats or animal blood were forbidden to Jews (Leviticus 7:20ff). But it may also be that Babylonian palace food was came from what was sacrificed to idols and represented to all concerned that this was participating in local idol worship. The young men drew the line here.

Notes on Question 4: How they stood up to their boss showed sensitivity to him and to company policy, which only made them seem more trustworthy. They asked for a test period to try out their win/win solution. They honored the goals set by management. They could keep their diet, but only if the results did not embarrass their boss with weakened workers. God honored their choice and the manner in which they negotiated with their boss.

Notes on Question 5: Daniel's friends were also his prayer team and personal board of directors for responding to challenges and hard choices, when to take a stand and when to yield. *(See also Daniel 2:17ff and 3:16-19, 6:10).* We learn in Daniel 6:10 that Daniel used to pray three times a day to his God. Praying alone and with his pals must have been the most sustaining of all God's resources. Prayer gave cohesion to all the other resources and tools God had given him. Prayer was their lifeline with God in their decision making day to day at work.

Notes on Question 6: What a variety of tools and resources God had given Daniel. physical appearance, brains, a reasonable boss, people skills, open doors of circumstances, a few friends who shared his faith in Yahweh, and an intimate relationship with the Lord of the Nations to help him integrate faith and daily life in Babylon.

Notes on Question 7: If you are feeling as though you are living in Babylon today, who are the friends who can pray with you as you seek to find your way through the complexities of living out your faith and making daily choices in a culture that constantly is pulling you off center? Be sure to thank them too for being your prayer partners and personal board of directors.

Notes on Question 8: The group might suggest some of the following actions: time with God in His Word and prayer (ACTS: Adoration, Confession, Thanksgiving, and Supplication); nurturing a friendship or prayer partner; journaling as you are waiting for God to act. Consider whom has God put in your life to help you work through issues at work. Ask God to give you wisdom through them. Ask God for discernment as you choose your next steps. Be sure to thank Him as you see Him work in your circumstances and for the discernment He gives you. But while waiting, just thank Him for who He is and for His presence with you.

Lesson 7

Working Alongside Difficult People

Introduction:

Perhaps nothing challenges our commitment to following Jesus more than difficult people, and this is especially true in our workplaces. We all have tales of bad bosses, obnoxious customers or clients and backstabbing coworkers. Not only do they make life miserable for us when they're around, but they also present a challenge to our faith. So how should Christian workers be equipped to resist the urge to bend their character when faced with these human resource nightmares? What steps can we take to resist reacting in a manner inconsistent with our faith?

Group Reflection:

What is the most challenging part of your job? What is the most challenging relationship on the job?

Individual Reflection:

What is your most challenging relationship at work and why? With whom do you find it easiest to work and why?

Read Nehemiah 4

1. Who are the people in Nehemiah's work life in this scene and what kind of relationship did Nehemiah have with each person or group?

2. What in particular did local leaders Sanballat and Tobiah do to make Nehemiah's life challenging?

3. How did Nehemiah respond to these difficult people with whom he had to work?

4. How did Nehemiah relate to and motivate his team of workers?

5. What are you learning from Nehemiah that will help you respond to the next conflict with a colleague at work?

6. What can you begin to do this week to change the way you respond to difficult people?

Prayer:

Teach me Jesus to see my colleagues as people you chose to die for and whom You are pursuing to come into relationship with You. Each one has been created in Your image and has the capacity to come to know You.

I give you . . . (names) . . . . And my relationship with him/her. By your Holy Spirit, give me insight into my words and actions that have contributed to any conflict. May my words and actions this week allow my colleagues to see Your character being lived out in me. If all he/she knows of You is from watching and interacting with me, may I more and more reflect your love, forgiveness and faithfulness in my relationships at work. I know there is more at stake than just getting my way.

Now or Later:

Observe in Nehemiah 1, Nehemiah's prayer life and how prayer influenced his life on the job in difficult situations.

For Leaders:

Notes on the Introduction: Most people find job skills easier to develop than the people skills needed to relate to different kinds of personalities in a competitive atmosphere where people often work in teams.

Notes on Question 1: In chapter 4, Nehemiah lived and worked in an arena of sustained hostility in Jerusalem. He is fighting for Israel's continuing spiritual existence in the 6th century BC. He was leading a team of workers who were discouraged (vs.10), fearful (vs.11) and vulnerable (vs.12). Nehemiah was having to choose how to respond to local power-players in Jerusalem, Sanballat and Tobiah, and also to those under their influence. Nehemiah offers some helpful "life ideas" even for us today.

For more information, read up on the background or characters in the *New Bible Dictionary* and/or The *New Bible Commentary* published by InterVarsity Press as cited in the Introduction to this study guide.

Notes on Question 2: Intimidation tactics from Sanballat and others were to ridicule and when that did not work, to bring in armed forces. Angry that their foothold of power and influence in Jerusalem would be undermined by the success of those returning from exile to rebuild their wall and the city, Sanballat and Tobiah mocked the ridiculous objective of Nehemiah and his team, the lack of resources, and their feeble incompetence. If Sanballat and Tobiah could immobilize Nehemiah and the returnees by creating self-doubt, the local leaders could continue to have economic and political control over the area. When verbal onslaughts did not work, they threatened to use their armed forces to accomplish it. We see two incidents of their intimidation tactics in this passage, and it will go on. Day in and day out, the stress can be wearing.

Notes on Question 3: Nehemiah models for us how to respond to angry intimidation tactics by those in power. Nehemiah first prays to God who is His ultimate boss and who has resourced him in amazing ways so far, before this crisis, as recorded in Nehemiah 1-3. Getting our focus on God and who He is, and what He has promised, and His faithfulness in the past has a way of creating a centered perspective. We see where the Holy Spirit, rather than our defensive anger, determines our next steps. Also, a correct focus increases our capacity to listen to God giving wisdom and creativity for our next steps. Nehemiah then asks for God to handle the revenge and justice issues (and perhaps his own anger) rather than to react out of anger himself. Releasing our anger and hurt into God's hands can clean up our motives to see whether we are just hurt and defensive or if we have righteous indignation. We are reminded by Jesus (Mark 3:5) and Paul the apostle (Ephesians 4:26, 31) that anger is not sin, but can often lead to it and leaves us vulnerable to poor judgment and harmful reactions. Justice is important but God's way of righting wrongs is also an important value to Nehemiah and to us. In addition, the second part of his response was to get back to work, rebuilding the wall. Nehemiah responded to the next aggressive intimidation tactic of Sanballat and Tobiah using physical force, first by focusing on God and then by addressing the weaknesses in their team's work and plan. Nehemiah was creative in adjusting the plan in light of the new obstacles. A guard was posted, manned by teams around the work area. They used the resources they had at hand.

Notes on Question 4: Motivating his team was also important to Nehemiah. He focused on two areas to help those around him not be immobilized by the intimidation tactics. First, that they were to remember who our God is, our ultimate boss, who is in charge here. Secondly, that they were to remember the people they cared about and were defending, their families, as they were all in this together. His attitude and actions were caught by the team. We do not make things happen for God at work, but we can partner with Him with through how we work and how we handle challenges. Keeping close contact with God will help shape our actions and our reactions, and let our human skills be in sync with God's agenda. When we understand that we exist to be in relationship with God, and that all we do serves that relationship, it becomes easier for us to turn to Him for help when faced with the weapons wielded by difficult people in our work lives.

Notes on Question 5: Two potential lessons are: First, the key to handling difficult people, overcoming criticism, resisting the discouragement that comes from ridicule, or living tentatively in the face of threats is to have an eternal focus that only comes from constant interaction with God. Secondly is to be willing to learn and change ones plans. God usually works through our human choices and plans. Just because we are seeking God's will, does not mean we have a corner on God's wisdom. Perhaps there is some wisdom to be learned from our critics.

Lesson 8

Avoiding Hype, Spin, and White Lies at Work

Introduction

What is the difference between an honest proposal and one that is an exaggeration? Does it make any difference if we leave early and put down a full day's hours the way others do? How do we communicate in this competitive culture in a way that pleases God? When we stretch a point on a resume (to get a hearing), is it really a lie? Can we call in sick and call it a personal day (still not having used up all allowable personal days yet)? What if we hold back information which would shape others' interpretation of the facts? Things have not changed much from King David's generation when he said, *"Help, LORD, for the godly are no more; the faithful have vanished from among men. Everyone lies to his neighbor; their flattering lips speak with deception."* (Psalm. 12:1ff). And what if we are on the receiving end of falsehoods? How should we respond? This is the culture we need to live and work in so how does God view the difference between unvarnished truth and adapting to our work cultures?

Group Reflection:

Why is telling the truth at work so hard for people, even though they do not want others to mislead them in hype and spin?

Individual Reflection:

When have you found it hard to tell the truth recently to someone? Why was it so difficult?

Read: Exodus 20:1-17, 23:1-9, and Matthew 15:17-20:

1. Read each of the Ten Commandments which God gave to Moses as basics for living. What does God say about lying or truth telling?

2. What is the relationship between lying or telling the truth with any of the other commandments?

3. How did God elaborate to Moses on the meaning of the 8th Commandment in Exodus 23:1-9?

4. What did Jesus say was the core issue in lying and telling the truth in Matthew 15:17-19?

5. What are the implications for business relationships? And personal relationships?

6. When people around the office tell lies and non-truths about you, how does Peter urge Christ-followers to respond? 1 Peter 2:12-24 writes to employees in his fellowship in the first century.

7. Think back on the incident you reflected on at the beginning of this lesson. If you could rewrite the script of how you would respond to the temptation to not tell the truth, what would it look like?

8. How might you respond if the spin and non-truth were focused on you?

Prayer:

Lord, I give you the situations at work and in my personal life where I feel challenged to speak or act truthfully. Give me wisdom to know how You want me to speak and act. Test my heart and transform it so I can hear you clearly speak by your Spirit.

May my words pass the test.

Now or Later:

Read in Matthew 6:9-13, The Lord's Prayer, and Colossians 3:7-17.

It will be easier for people to hear "tough news", if our relationships have been consistently marked by kindness, wisdom that proves true, and team building at work. A helpful acronym as we think about words we want to speak whether at home or work is **THINK.**

T Is it true?
H Is it helpful?
I Is it inspiring?
N Is it nurturing?
K Is it kind?

For Leaders:

Notes on Questions 1, 2 and 3: From the time of Moses, truth-telling was a challenge for God's people as they sought to follow God in real life. Not lying about others (Exodus 20:16) made it into the Ten Commandments because God values each individual's true character. In that culture character was a person's most valuable commodity. Words were taken seriously both in business contracts and personal promises. God took people's words seriously too. Elaborations in Exodus 23:1ff tell us that truth telling in civil and business relationships is important to God. We learn that not even sympathy for the poor should sway justice in the courts.

Notes on Question 4 and 5: If God has designed us to be truth tellers, and since Jesus has taken up residence in our lives, at the core of our being, why isn't telling the truth easier for us? Why isn't it the first response in our fast paced, pressure packed days? Jesus tells us that from God's perspective, telling the truth is primarily a heart issue. (Matthew 15:17ff). Our words reflect our deepest values. The bigger our God, the more we can trust Him with our total wellbeing. When tempted to control or manipulate our circumstances, Jesus wants us to remember: God keeps His promises to look out for our wellbeing. God is going to protect us when we are threatened. God is the one who will revenge/punish wrongs, can see through lies of ours or others. God can provide for us better than we can ourselves. God will always have the last word in our lives and that of others. If the heart is the main issue, then the main solution is to keep filled with the Holy Spirit from 9am to 5pm. Lying sabotages our walk with the Spirit. It is a short term quick fix but a long-term war against our souls.

Notes on Question 6: What if people are telling lies or non-truths about us around the office? How should we respond? God tells us through Peter as he writes about following Christ in the public arena, *"I urge you, as aliens and strangers in the world, to abstain from sinful desires, which war against your soul. Live such good lives among the pagans that, though they accuse you of doing wrong, they may see your good deeds and glorify God on the day he visits us."*

(1 Peter 2:12ff.) Peter talks about heart condition issues too, things that war against our souls. But Peter says there is another important issue that should help shape our responses to those who say things about us that are not true. *"To this you were called, because Christ suffered for you, leaving you an example, that you should follow in his steps. 'He committed no sin, and no deceit was found in his mouth'. When they hurled their insults at him, he did not retaliate; when he suffered, he made no threats. Instead, he entrusted himself to him who judges justly".*

Notes on Questions 7 and 8: Our first response could be to "give it back to them" in verbal defense to get even. But if we counted to 10 and gave the lie to God to evaluate and help us respond, it might give God a communication tool in the very person's life who hurt us. Peter says it is not about us. It is all about God and His agenda. How can God be glorified by my response today to this lie about me? The answer may not be immediate. I may not even see a favorable outcome, but the test comes when Jesus comes again or when a person goes to meet Jesus. Did the way we responded make it easier for them to give Jesus a hearing when He seeks to visit them?

What if we gave the falsehood to God, went to the person who hurt us, and asked what they meant by what was said? Besides diffusing the situation, preserving the relationship through talking through conflict, we might even change the office culture one life at a time. An investment manager was deprived of any credit for work done for a couple of years by the person's boss. Several years later when both were at new companies they ran into each other at an industry conference. The former boss came to her to tell her he had become a Christian and wanted her to know that he was very grateful for what she had modeled for him. The new humility in this new child of God, in her former boss, was great reward for trusting Jesus with the lack of truth-telling several years before.

Let's live today in a way that Jesus will say in our ultimate Annual Review, "Well done you good and faithful servant. You have been faithful in the little things like truth telling. Now I want to trust you with something new."

Lesson 9

Walking The Talk at Work

Introduction

The Fraud Triangle is a term coined by Stephen Albrecht in his research of business ethics. He presented his findings in the book, *Fraud: Bringing Light to the Dark Side of Business* (1994). He was surprised to discover that the $40 to $60 billion per year of employee fraud is 16 times more likely to be committed by managers and executives; and 5 times more likely to be committed by employees who have post-graduate degrees. The more pressure to measure success by what we own, wear, drive, and do, the more fraud happens Albrecht found. *The Fraud Triangle* is often described by crime specialists as (1) a real or perceived need that causes employees to look for ways to ease their fiscal pressures; (2) the opportunity to commit fraud; and (3) the ability to rationalize the behavior. Looking at the family of the patriarch Isaac reminds us of how vulnerable all humans are, including those who claim to be followers of our holy God. Family cultures and corporate cultures have much in common in their effect on individual choices.

Group Reflection:

When have you been surprised by the unethical behavior of a successful business person or of a person who claims to follow Christ?

Individual Reflection:

When have you personally found yourself rationalizing your unethical behavior? Or have strongly been tempted to?

Read Genesis 25:27-34 and 27:2-24

1. What were some of the things Jacob did to get what he wanted?

2. What were some of the things Esau and Rebekah each did to get what they wanted?

3. What were the consequences in the family relationships and the "family business"?

   a. For Esau?

   b. For Rebekah?

   c. For Jacob, one of the three patriarchs of Israel, a mentor and leadership model?

4. What are some "preventative health" measures they each could have taken to avoid their unethical choices?

5. What deep desires drive you in life? In what area of life are you most likely to run ahead of God to get what you want?

Prayer:

Lord, I give you the deep desires of my heart and life that seem essential to my happiness. I give them to you to clean up, change or fulfill to your glory. I name them before you now . . . .

Now or Later:

Read 1 Timothy 6 and consider some of Paul's suggestions to the young leader, Timothy, for preventative health measures?

Practice a few Bridge Building Questions in Appendix C.

For Leaders:

Notes on Question 1: What were some of the things Jacob was willing to do to get what he wanted? In Genesis 25:27ff, we find the twin sons of Isaac showing their characters as young men. The eldest twin had the birthright of inheriting the family CEO position and double financial inheritance over other siblings. Esau, the father's favorite, seemed to be more influenced by his immediate physical needs than the position of family leader. As the grandson of Abraham, his position made him also the fulfiller of God's promises to bless the entire human race through his family as descendents of Abraham (Gen. 12:1ff). Jacob, second in line, was so eager to get the position of family CEO, that he took advantage of his twin brother's hunger and impetuousness, and asked Esau to pay for the lentil stew with his birthright. Jacob in a premeditated way knew how to take advantage of his brother's vulnerabilities. God had promised before their birth that the elder would be ruled by the younger (Gen.25:19ff), but Jacob (means "Grabber) did not want to wait or trust God. To get what he wanted, Jacob was willing to take any shortcut.

Notes on Question 2: Rebekah was willing to lie to her husband and eldest son to get her favorite child to receive the family blessing of top position in family estate and decision making, along with a double financial bonus. She helped create a culture of deception and lying. (Genesis 27:2ff) Esau was willing to commit murder to get what he wanted and what his culture said he deserved as eldest son. He was willing to murder his twin brother.

Notes on Question 3: The consequence was a family in conflict and grief for decades. Rebecca coached Jacob on deceptive tactics. The collateral damage in the family was conflict in marriage, in extended family relationships, attempted murder by Esau, and patterns of behavior that followed the two boys and their parents for the rest of their lives. The short-term perceived need turned into long-term disappointments in the extended family. The promise of God to Abraham to bless the entire world through his descendents would have been lost, if not for a grace giving God who loves to redeem our failures if we just turn around and let Him onto the decision making throne of our lives.

Notes on Question 4: Preventative health measures to deal with our real or potential temptations:

1. Bring to God our real or potential Fraud Triangles: our perceived or real needs as we seek to deal with our pressure packed lives and a marketing culture that seduces daily;

2. Keep short accounts with God by confession of failures regularly.

3. Bring to God and a good friend the opportunities to commit fraud that we face day to day. Consider having a Personal Board of Directors with whom to review major decisions or vulnerable areas of your life.

4. Pray through our choices in light of God's Word to help understand when we are rationalizing our behavior. A personal board of directors whom we check in with regularly will help hold us accountable, and they will pray for us, particularly in our vulnerable areas. They can help to keep us honest with God and with ourselves.

Lesson 10

Talking About God in a Secular Environment

Introduction

How do we find natural opportunities to talk about God that are appropriate to our marketplace environment? What will keep our conversation about Jesus from being marginalized? When Paul arrived in Athens in the first century, he was asking the same question. Apparently there were no followers of Christ there. Paul had to work from "the outside in". Paul addressed the "Greeks" in three very different settings in Athens: the Jewish meeting place (synagogue), the Areopagus (the supreme council), and the agora or marketplace. This required three different approaches, and it shows something of Paul's great ability to communicate. He always started where people were.

Group Reflection:

As you listen to people around you and as you read advertisements, what is on people's hearts and mind? What things do they want to talk about? And what do they spend their time and money on?

Individual Reflection:

What first attracted you to become a believer and follower of Jesus as an adult? What was your natural gateway of interest? How has Jesus made a difference in your life recently?

Read Acts 17:13-34

1. What was Paul's first impression as he arrived in Athens?

2. What needed to happen in Paul's life before he could begin to relate to the Athenians?

3. What different groups of people did Paul address and relate to in Athens?

4. In what ways was his interaction with each group the same? How was it different?

5. Looking at the agora or town meeting place, what natural pathways did Paul tap into as he began to converse with the people?

6. What progression do you notice in his dialogue with them?

7. What interests do you notice that others have that could lead you into a conversation about Jesus?

8. When did Jesus become more than just a name to you and who or what helped that to happen?

9. Is there anything about your behavior or talents that would cause others to ask about your beliefs?

10. Is there anything about your behavior that would compromise your witness?

Prayer:

Thank you God that I do not have to make conversations happen about You at work. Give me eyes to see what you are doing at work in my colleagues. Give me ears to hear what questions my colleagues have or what issues really engage their minds and attention. Holy Spirit, teach me to partner with you at work in what you are doing in the lives of my colleagues.

Now or Later:

Observe how Jesus began and developed a dialogue with an unlikely person in John 4:6ff. How did he start the conversation? How did he handle arguments? How did Jesus use questions to open up dialogue or move it along?

For Leaders:

Suggestions on Group and Individual Reflection:

As you listen to people around you and as you read advertisements, here a *few good questions* to ask, as you seek to find gateways into what is on people's hearts and minds, things they want to talk about.

- What do people talk about over lunch together?
- How do people spend their time and money?
- What are people dreaming about, thinking about, and longing for?
- How do people make sense out of life?

Notes on Question 1: Having been kicked out of Berea and Thessalonica, Paul was brought to Athens for safety and to be picked up for his next journey. Exhausted, unwelcome in most places by people in leadership, he arrived in Athens where he has no support system. He was greatly distressed by the religious idolatry all over the city.

Notes on Question 2: Paul had to move beyond being overwhelmed by his first impressions of Athens. Paul could have reacted to the secular and religious pluralism, or to the constant rejection by so many in previous cities, but he chose to respond to the God of the Nations he had come to know who was omnipotent, omnipresent, and omniscient. God had called him to be a presenter of the good news about Jesus to those who do not yet know Him. Then he could start thinking about what was going on in the hearts and minds of those he met, as opposed to how he was feeling about himself and how he was being perceived by others.

Notes on Question 3: We see Paul conversing with people in Athens based on what he observed to be natural gateways for them. For the synagogue crowd, he reasoned from the Old Testament scriptures. When in the secular arena of the Areopagus (philosophers and the governing council), he affirmed the religious pluralism, their local poets, and one of the many altars in the public square "To an Unknown God". Paul then moved the conversation to the next level. He had been asked to speak but had not forced the opportunity. They had heard about Paul and his new worldview and were curious. The response was mixed. The next level of conversation was also by invitation, to understand more about the content of his faith, Jesus and the resurrection. We know of at least one council member who became a follower of Jesus, Dionysius, and a few other listeners.

So how do we start where people are and know how to move the conversation to the next level? Some people will watch us and ask us questions about how our faith makes a difference in our lives, such as walking through hard times or some area they have observed. Sometimes we can share from our life experience, how God has helped us cope, change, overcome something. But we can also ask questions. Most people like to talk about themselves and have someone take an interest in them.

Notes on Question 7: Think up a few questions to ask which will open up the conversation with a colleague, on an area of interest to them. Ask the Holy Spirit to be your teacher as you listen, observe, and think up possible questions. We want to partner with the Holy Spirit and what He is doing in people's lives.

The topics frequently identified as gateways in our various offices and relationships are:

- Moral compass—expectations of integrity, fairness, and excellence in how we are treated,
- Inner turmoil—unhappiness on the job, lay-offs, difficult relationships at work or home
- Personal tragedy—illness, death
- Relationships—loneliness, how to grow and keep relationships, lack of caring for others at work
- Cultural drift—what values people consider important
- Security—economic, relational, physical
- Meaning in life
- Contentment
- Current reading—articles, books, films,

Is there any connection between these topics and your path to Jesus?

If so, this might help build bridges and find common interests.

Appendices

Appendix A: Finding Meaning in Work

Principles

1. To enjoy our work is a gift from God which He deeply desires to give to us.

2. Work is an opportunity for the expression of Christ in us.

Key Perspectives

1. Purpose in Life: The first question is not how to fit God into my plans, but how my life fits into God's plan.

2. Congruence: Work becomes meaningful as my heart and actions are aligned with God's designs and plans.

3. Source of Meaning: We don't derive meaning from our work; we bring meaning to it.

4. Life Giving Perspective: The perspective I bring to work can either be life-giving or life draining. I must develop a life-giving perspective of my work to bring meaning to it.

5. Inside-out: We bring meaning to our work (life) as we live from the inside-out vs. from the outside-in.

6. Identity: Who I am is not determined by what I do. Rather, what I do is an expression of who I am.

7. Meaning in the moment: Meaning is found in the moment not in the memories of the past or our plans for the future. The only opportunity I have to express myself is right here, right now.

8. Undulation: Life has its inevitable ups and downs. Growth and meaning are found in embracing the highs and lows.

Barry L. Rowan, from an unpublished seminar 1996

Appendix B: There Are No Ordinary People

Meanwhile the cross comes before the crown and tomorrow is a Monday morning. A cleft has opened in the pitiless walls of the world, and we are invited to follow our great Captain inside. The following Him is, of course, the essential point. That being so, it may be asked what practical use there is in the speculations, which I have been indulging. I can think of at least one such use. It may be possible for each to think too much of his own potential glory hereafter; it is hardly possible for him to think too often or too deeply about that of his neighbor. The load, or weight, or burden of my neighbor's glory should be laid on my back, a load so heavy that only humility can carry it, and the backs of the proud will be broken. It is a serious thing to live in a society of possible gods and goddesses, to remember that the dullest and most uninteresting person you can talk to may one day be a creature which, if you say it now, you would be strongly tempted to worship, or else a horror and a corruption such as you now meet, if at all, only in a nightmare. All day long we are, in some degree, helping each other to one or other of these destinations. It is in the light of these overwhelming possibilities, it is with the awe and the circumspection proper to them, that we should conduct all our dealings with one another, all friendships, all loves, all play, all politics. There are no ordinary people. You have never talked to a mere mortal. Nations, cultures, arts, civilizations—these are mortal, and their life is to ours as the life of a gnat. But it is immortals with whom we joke with, work with, marry, snub, and exploit—immortal horrors or everlasting splendors. This does not mean that we are to be perpetually solemn. We must play. But our merriment, must be of that kind (and it is, in fact, the merriest kind) which exists between people who have, from the outset, taken each other seriously—no flippancy, no superiority, no presumption. And our charity must be a real and costly love, with deep feeling for the sins in spite of which we love the sinner—no mere tolerance, or indulgence which parodies love as flippancy parodies merriment. Next to the Blessed Sacrament itself, your neighbor is the holiest object Presented to your senses. If he is your Christian neighbor, he is holy in almost the same way, for in him also Christ *vere latitat*-the glorifier and he glorified, Glory Himself, is truly hidden.

---

[1] *(C.S Lewis, Weight of Glory, New York: MacMillan, 1965, p. 18-19)*

Appendix C: Bridge Building Questions

Meaning and purpose

- What do you most enjoy about your work? Your life?
- What do you find challenging about your work? About your life?
- How do you find meaning and purpose in your life?
- If you could change one thing in your life, what would it be?

Relationships

- What is your family like? If you could change one thing about your family and how you were raised, what would it be?
- What do you think contributes to a good relationship?
- What exposure to faith did you have in childhood?
- Tell me something about how your faith began?
- What helps loving relationships to happen? What causes trust to develop between two people?
- Do you think people can change? What might cause a person to change?
- Do you think lasting love is a possibility between two people?
- What ingredients are necessary for love to grow?

Going through hard times

- Does your faith provide meaning or help for what you are going through?
- Has it ever occurred to you to ask God for help?

Views on Christianity and Christians

- What kind of a church would ever interest you?
- What advice would you give to Christians?
- Whom do you admire and why?
- Who is Jesus Christ in your opinion?
- When you think of God or a Supreme Being, what do you think of?
- Can this Being be known personally? How?
- Would you ever want to visit a church with me this Lenten season?

Interests

- Think about a favorite movie or book: What character did you find yourself most drawn to and why?
- I am curious as to why you think . . .
- I am wondering how you came to feel so strongly about, or be convinced that . . .